Original title:
Pluto's Poetry Party

Copyright © 2025 Creative Arts Management OÜ
All rights reserved.

Author: Beckett Sinclair
ISBN HARDBACK: 978-1-80567-830-4
ISBN PAPERBACK: 978-1-80567-951-6

## Rhapsody in Cosmic Blue

In a nebula strummed by comets bright,
The stars giggle in the velvet night.
A dancing asteroid spins a tale,
While moonbeams twinkle, without fail.

Jupiter's moons play hide and seek,
While Martians plot their next mystique.
The sun wakes up with a cheeky grin,
And cosmic winds invite us in.

Saturn's rings can't help but sway,
With space dust miming a cabaret.
Galaxies toast with cosmic cheer,
As laughter echoes through the sphere.

Floating far, a joke takes flight,
A black hole whispers, "What's the light?"
Stars wink, sharing quirky schemes,
In a universe knitted from dreams.

# The Invisible Poet's Quill

A poet scribbles in the void,
With words that dance and can't be buoyed.
He laughs at comets, mocks their trails,
In cosmic realms where whimsy sails.

With ink made from starlit dew,
His verses twinkle, bright and new.
Red giants chuckle, blue dwarfs tease,
As stardust floats on cosmic breeze.

An alien laughs, shakes with glee,
As rhymes spin round in zero-G.
The sun blushes at a pun so bad,
It sends the aliens all quite mad.

Across the sky, jokes take their flight,
Galactic chuckles fill the night.
A meteoric laugh, a cosmic thrill,
All thanks to the invisible poet's quill.

## Echoes of a Forgotten Realm

In a land where icebergs sing,
The penguin dons a golden ring.
He twirls and slides on frosty floors,
Cracking jokes with snowflake corps.

A walrus with a shiny mustache,
Recites rhymes that make the ice smash.
The seals all giggle, shivering delight,
As laughter echoes through the night.

While comets flash a chilly grin,
We toast with cups of frozen gin.
Galactic parties, stars galore,
In this realm, who could ask for more?

Let's dance on the rings of Saturn's flair,
With cosmic tunes that fill the air.
Jupiter joins with a trumpet blast,
In this forgotten land, fun is unsurpassed.

## The Soul of a Frigid World

Frosty breezes twist and twine,
As penguins dance in perfect line.
A polar bear with shades on tight,
Sips hot cocoa, what a sight!

Icicles hang like laughing dolls,
While snowmen tell their towering tales.
The Arctic fox, with mismatched socks,
Leading a troupe of silly flocks.

A seal juggles fish with flair,
While the night sky plays fair.
Stars wink down, they're in on the jest,
In this frigid world, we feel so blessed.

Snowballs fly with giggly glee,
In the winter sun, come dance with me!
Mirthful moments, frosty air,
In this realm, there's joy to share.

**Cosmic Conversations in Stillness**

Amongst the stars, a chat unfolds,
A cactus claims to know the cold.
With witty lines, it jabs the moon,
While Saturn hums a playful tune.

Asteroids crash, but laugh it off,
One claims it's just a silly scoff.
As meteors whiz with blazing trails,
Conversations spin like comet sails.

The sun joins in with radiant flair,
Chimes in with warmth, it's fair to share.
Galactic gossip flies like sparks,
As planets gossip about the sharks.

In the quiet void, laughter rings,
Echoes of joy from cosmic things.
Together we dance, in stellar bliss,
In this stillness, how could we miss?

## Chronicles of Space's Fringe

On the edge of galaxies untold,
A mouse astronaut spins tales bold.
With cheese-shaped stars lighting the way,
He dances under the Milky Way.

Aliens toast with cups of goo,
Saying, "Earthlings are quite a crew!"
While a green blob does the robot zap,
In this corner, the cosmos takes a nap.

Neptune throws a giant ball,
Where space whales sing and dolphins call.
The party's buzzing, and it's a thrill,
In the fringes, time stands still.

So come on down to the cosmic soiree,
Where laughter rolls like waves at play.
For in these chronicles, joy we find,
In the universe's embrace, we're intertwined.

## In the Company of Celestial Giants

In a realm where giants spin,
They dance on stars with silly grin.
With cosmic snacks and jokes so bright,
They giggle through the endless night.

Uranus tells a joke so grand,
While Saturn laughs, a wobbly band.
Mars throws confetti, what a sight!
Even comets join in the light.

Jupiter's thunder roars with glee,
While Venus rolls like a tumbleweed.
Neptune claims he's the best at chess,
But loses to a starry mess.

So gather round, let laughter reign,
In this cosmic waltz, there's no disdain.
With big balloon suns and silly hats,
The universe chuckles, and how it chats!

## Beyond Neptune's Gaze

Far beyond where the sunlight fades,
Lies a place of jumbled charades.
Stars play hide and seek with delight,
While comets race at the speed of light.

A dancing asteroid skips along,
Singing off-key a celestial song.
Jupiter's moon tosses pies in the air,
With Saturn's rings providing flair.

Neptune giggles at the absurd,
While transiting worlds seem undeterred.
With laughter echoing through the void,
Space shenanigans can't be destroyed!

So raise a toast to the night so bright,
To all the worlds that spin with delight.
For each twinkling light holds a story to share,
In this whimsical land, there's fun everywhere!

## A Lullaby for Lost Worlds

Hush now, listen to the starry sighs,
Lost worlds dreaming beneath the skies.
Whispers of laughter float on by,
As cosmic crickets chirp, oh my!

A sleepy planet with a fuzzy face,
Swings gently in the cosmic race.
While meteors drift like dreamers' ships,
Painting the night with comical quips.

Rings of Saturn sway in the breeze,
Joining in tune with the teasing trees.
Uranus snores, while moons giggle soft,
Cradled in stardust, dreams take off.

So close your eyes and count the stars,
Imagine the fun of cosmic avatars.
With laughter sprinkled in the dark,
These lost worlds cradle a playful spark!

## Anthems of the Far Out

Gather round for an anthem, you bet,
From moons and planets you won't forget.
In the vortex of space, with humor and cheer,
Comets join in, their voices so clear.

As the stars shake hands, the fun unwinds,
With jokes about galaxies left behind.
Neptune croons, and Titan strums,
While goofy satellites dance and hums.

Beyond the rings, there's giggling fun,
Chasing meteoric rays from the sun.
In the cosmic hall, where laughter rolls,
Each voice echoes like distant trolls.

So sing along in the stellar light,
Let the far-out tunes take you to flight.
For in the heart of the galaxy's play,
An anthem of joy echoes night and day!

## Lullabies of Enigmatic Orbits

In the dark where comets play,
Stars trade jokes at the end of day.
A dancing moon in silly hats,
Whispers secrets to the cats.

Asteroids spin, it's quite a sight,
Riding on beams of pure moonlight.
With giggles echoing through the night,
Galaxies twirl in pure delight.

## The Playground of Celestial Bodies

Swinging high on Saturn's rings,
Playing tag with the cosmic flings.
Uranus laughs as Neptune spins,
While Venus grins at their silly sins.

Jupiter jumps, a big round ball,
Mars plays tag and bounces tall.
While Earth giggles, spinning 'round,
In this playground of joy, we're found.

**Verses in the Shadow of Giants**

Underneath the gaze of greats,
Tiny worlds spin and debate fates.
With a wink, the dwarf stars beam,
In this twilight, we all seem.

Giggles flow through cosmic dust,
Orbiting giants, we all must.
Space is a stage for silly dreams,
Where laughter echoes in moonlit beams.

## Echoes of a Forgotten Planet

Once a world, now just a tale,
Winking quietly beneath the veil.
It tells jokes in a raspy tone,
A cheeky spirit, forever alone.

In whispers soft as stardust dreams,
It chuckles at life's silly schemes.
A party still in echoes' sway,
Where laughter lingers, night and day.

## **Twilight Whispers of the Kuiper Belt**

In shadows cast by icy rocks,
We gather 'round with laughter's knocks.
A comet's tail, a wobbly dance,
And all the stars just steal a glance.

With jokes that orbit every star,
We toast to quirks from near and far.
Each chuckle echoes through the night,
As laughter flickers, pure delight.

A moonbeam spills its silver glow,
While little asteroids join the show.
With cosmic snacks and playful cheer,
We spin our tales, no need for fear.

So raise a cup of starlit juice,
To every twinkle, bright and loose.
In Kuiper's maze, we find our way,
With humor's spark to light the day.

**Galactic Gatherings of the Heart**

From Venus' smiles to Mars' jokes,
We float on dreams like silly folks.
Uranus laughs, a cheeky sight,
Saturn's rings spin with pure delight.

A rocket's fuel, just giggles and glee,
Dancing comets, wild and free.
Each supernova bursts with cheer,
As stellar friends gather near.

Galaxies whirl in a playful spree,
Galactic games for you and me.
We trade our puns like cosmic dust,
In laughter's glow, we all adjust.

So let's unite in joyful mirth,
For here's the place of cosmic birth.
In this gathering, we'll always find,
The heart's own glow, hilariously kind.

## Poems at the Edge of the Universe

At the frontier where stars collide,
We scribble verse, with joy and pride.
Nebulae bloom with funny rhymes,
In orbit, we play with silly chimes.

We pen our tales of purple screams,
While black holes yawning chew our dreams.
With every verse, the cosmos sways,
And all of space is in a daze.

Asteroids chuckle, comets tease,
As we write poetry with ease.
On distant worlds, we spread delight,
As galaxies giggle through the night.

So come along, don't be shy,
With every line, we shoot for the sky.
At the edge of all that's known,
We find the laughter we can own.

## The Secret Life of Celestial Nomads

Nomads drifting through the void,
With tales of mischief, well deployed.
A starry wink, a cosmic grin,
In every world, we wear the fin.

We wander through the space-time fold,
Trading stories, brave and bold.
Jupiter's storms, a laugh or two,
As Saturn shows his dance debut.

With playful pranks we sail the night,
In every twinkle, pure delight.
Galaxy hopping with great flair,
We throw confetti through the air.

So join our crew of cosmic jest,
With every laugh, we feel the best.
Together we'll explore the skies,
With silly dreams that never die.

## IS Shadowed Verse of the Dwarf

In the dark where shadows play,
Rhyme and reason drift away.
A tiny planet, proud and petite,
Crafting verses, oh so sweet.

Stars are giggling, planets dance,
In the void, they take a chance.
A comet sneezes, sending flights,
Of wacky words on starry nights.

Whispers echo, laughter loud,
In cosmos where we're all so proud.
A dwarf in space, with great desire,
To spin a tale that will inspire.

Yet here we are, the jokes fly by,
As asteroids roll, and meteors cry.
In each little quirk, we find our flair,
A cosmic party, without a care.

## Musings from the Cosmic Kettle

From the kettle, stars are brewed,
Cosmic soup and laughter stewed.
Aliens pour with silly glee,
Mixing rhymes for you and me.

A pinch of comets, a dash of light,
Sprinkle stardust, oh what a sight!
Galactic jokes in every sip,
Take a taste, let laughter rip!

Tea with Martians, cakes from Mars,
We feast on dreams, sipping stars.
The Milky Way twirls with delight,
In the kettle, we brew the night.

Quantum giggles stir the brew,
With space-time tumblings, it's all askew.
So grab your cups, let's drink away,
In the cosmic kettle, we laugh and play!

## Twilight Tales of the Far Reaches

In twilight's grasp, where tales unfold,
Adventures lurk, both quirky and bold.
A starry wiggle, a wobbly dance,
Cosmic stories put you in a trance.

Far reaches of space, we giggle and roam,
With tales of aliens, far from home.
A clumsy Martian trips on a moon,
While Saturn rings play a silly tune.

In this night sky, we dream and laugh,
As supernovae send their autograph.
A joke from Uranus, a roar from the sun,
Twilight tales are shared, oh what fun!

So gather 'round, my cosmic friends,
Let's spin some yarns that never end.
In the vastness, there's joy to find,
Twilight whispers to the wandering mind.

## Interstellar Rhythms

Bouncing beats from star to star,
In the dark, we twirl and spar.
Rhythms echo, rockets zoom,
In the vastness, there's always room.

Planets dance, with wobble and sway,
To the music of the Milky Way.
Galaxies giggle, asteroids roll,
In this funky space, we find our soul.

Interstellar tunes play a tune,
Singing to the bright green moon.
Each note a comet, each beat a sun,
In this rhythm, we've all won!

So join the band, let laughter ring,
In the cosmos, we dance and sing.
With beats from afar, we'll never tire,
Interstellar rhythms, lift us higher!

## Celestial Verses of the Dwarf World

In the dark of space, a tiny ball,
With a grin so wide, it stands so small.
Dwarfs in the cosmos, dancing around,
They bounce with joy, not a frown to be found.

Giggles echo in the Milky Way,
As they juggle stars in a comical play.
With moons as partners, they twirl and spin,
A celestial circus where all can win.

They sip on stardust, sweet as pie,
And share the tales of the bright night sky.
Each joke is a planet, each laugh is a star,
In this humorous realm, they shine from afar.

So come join the fun, no need to be shy,
In this little world where laughter can fly.
With a wink and a nod, come dance in the light,
In the chin-up cosmos, everything's bright.

## Cosmic Rhymes Beneath the Ice

Beneath the frost, where the cold winds blow,
A frost-covered world puts on quite the show.
Icebergs giggle, whispering charm,
While comets and asteroids keep them warm.

They craft a tale of a big snowball,
Carved from dreams, it's a whimsical call.
With every roll, they dance and glide,
In this winter wonderland, laughter's our guide.

The starlight chuckles, twinkling so bright,
As the space-folk gather for a cosmic night.
They play silly games of tag and chase,
In the frozen realm, there's joy to embrace.

So gather around for a giggly cheer,
In this icy haven, there's nothing to fear.
With hiccups of joy, let the stories unfold,
In this frosty place, where laughter turns gold.

## Whispers from the Edge of the Solar Sea

At the edge of our system, whispers abound,
Where waves of stardust crash on the ground.
Each ripple giggles, each splash sings a rhyme,
Creating a symphony beyond space and time.

Aliens lounge on soft cosmic sand,
With drinks made of light, they form a band.
They strum on meteors, beat on the tides,
In the galactic beach party, joy never hides.

They tell tales of comets that bumble and crash,
While stars shoot by with a wink and a flash.
Each wave giggles, each breeze has a tease,
In this silly ocean, smiles are the keys.

So join in the fun, let your worries cease,
In the cosmic surf, we find our peace.
With laughter and light from the farthest place,
We dance with the stars, in this endless space.

## Starlit Sonnets of the Farthest Realm

In the distant void, where the giggles grow,
Lies a realm of wonders, where funny faces glow.
Stars wear sunglasses, moons pout and pose,
In this zany universe, humor overflows.

From being a planet to a jesting dwarf,
Each celestial body finds its comedic course.
With quips and puns, they frolic with glee,
In their cosmic cabaret, come sing with me.

They tell silly stories through meteor showers,
Sprinkling humor like the finest of flowers.
With laughter that dances through the vacuum of night,
In the farthest domain, everything feels right.

So twirl with the comets, sway with the rays,
Join the starlit sonnets, let laughter blaze.
In this funny galaxy, let your spirit soar,
For joy is the theme, and we all want more!

## Comets and Sonnets

In the sky, comets dance,
They wear their tails with flair.
Sonnets float on cosmic winds,
A rhyming burst of air.

Stars giggle as they twinkle,
Planets spin in glee.
A meteor takes a bow,
If you will, come see!

Cosmic jokes in starlit skies,
We laugh until we cry.
Gravity might pull us down,
But we aim to fly high!

Verse by verse, the universe,
Creates its own sweet song.
With each beat, we find our feet,
And dance where we belong.

## Infinity's Quiet Narratives

In the void, stories linger,
Whispers dance in space.
Asteroids play hide and seek,
With a cosmic wink and grace.

Galaxies spin tales of laughter,
Stars chuckle, a bright glee.
The black holes hum a tune,
Of mysteries we can't see.

Nebulas glow in pastel hues,
Clouds of thought so light.
Each pixel of the night sky,
Is a punchline wrapped in fright!

So come and share a secret,
With the cosmos as our stage.
Infinity's a quiet friend,
Let's play with words like sage.

## Ballads from the Dark Side of the Cosmos

On the dark side, moonlight giggles,
With shadows that sway and glide.
Planets strum their silent strings,
While comets wink with pride.

Black holes spin their yarns of gloom,
But laughter's always near.
A chorus echoes through the void,
It sings while we all cheer.

Asteroids tapdance on the rings,
With meteors on cue.
Every twinkling star is bright,
But none outshine this crew!

So hear the ballads of the night,
As galaxies unite.
In this grand and funny show,
We find our pure delight.

## Frozen Fables of the Night Sky

Under blankets, stars are sleeping,
Cold tales drift and slide.
The moon plays hide and seek with dreams,
While laughter's tucked inside.

Fables wrapped in winter's chill,
Tell stories of the bright.
With every twinkle in the sky,
A giggle sparks the night.

Meteor showers bring the jokes,
In a flicker, they thrive.
Each moment sparkles with delight,
As cosmic beings jive!

So gather 'round the starlit tales,
Let humor be our guide.
In frozen fables, we rejoice,
And let our hearts collide.

## Frosted Dreams in the Frozen Expanse

In the chill where comets play,
The snowflakes dance in a merry ballet.
A snowman waves, with a carrot snout,
Singing tunes that make starlights shout!

With igloos made of cosmic cream,
Aliens giggle, sharing a dream.
Hot cocoa flows through the icy space,
As marshmallow meteors race in the race!

Laughter echoes through ice-cold nights,
While frosty friends love starry sights.
They throw snowballs of frozen light,
In a galaxy that sparkles bright!

So raise a glass of frozen cheer,
To frosted dreams that bring us near.
In the frozen expanse, we spark our glee,
In this cosmic party, just you and me!

## The Melancholy of Distant Moons

Oh, lonely moons in the darkened sky,
Spinning tales of love that make us sigh.
With a frown, they orbit, feeling quite blue,
Wishing for a dance partner, too!

They gather dust from cosmic woes,
Making craters where all sorrow goes.
A wink from a comet cheers one up,
"Why not join the interstellar cup?"

Stars twinkle with mischief, begin to tease,
"Join the laughter, bring the freeze!"
So the moons, once sad, start to sway,
Shaking off woes in a blissful ballet!

From depths of gloom, they burst in a whirl,
Cosmic confetti starts to twirl.
The melancholy fades in joyful light,
As laughter echoes through the starry night!

## **Rhythms of the Outer Frontier**

In the vacuum where silence reigns,
A funky beat takes the cosmic chains.
Asteroids jam with a funky flair,
While rockets spin in the swirling air!

Quasars groove, flickering bright,
In this dance-off of immaculate light.
Planets bop to rhythms alive,
With the universe's hit jive!

Martian mimes juggle rings of dust,
With lunar lollipops, it's a must!
Galactic dancers spin in delight,
As they shuffle past the stars at night!

So let's waltz in this outer space,
To celestial tunes, we'll find our place.
With laughter and rhythm, come take my hand,
In the outer frontier, we shall stand!

## Notes from the Ninth

On the edge of the cosmic sway,
Where whispers of laughter blow away.
Jazz notes echo from frosty spheres,
Tickling our toes, dissolving fears!

A symphony played with icy keys,
While frozen statues giggle with ease.
Candyfloss comets swirl with a snap,
As we all settle into this lap!

Those little stars wink with glee,
Joining the jolly jubilee.
In this cold realm, we warm our souls,
With harmonies that make us whole!

So grab your hats and icy strings,
Let the joy of the ninth one sings.
In this laughter-filled night so grand,
We pen our notes, hand in hand!

## **Interstellar Poetry from the Twilight Zone**

In a realm where the planets all dance,
The aliens munch on a cosmic cheese France.
They rhyme about stars with silly delight,
And sing with great joy through the day and the night.

A black hole hiccups, and planets all spin,
They giggle and laugh, let the games now begin.
With meteors juggling and comets that prank,
Each poem a party, a cosmic prank bank.

Asteroids twirl with a curious grace,
While rockets tell jokes about interstellar space.
They rhyme through the void, where the giggles collide,
On the stage of the cosmos, there's nowhere to hide.

So grab your space pen and take to the floor,
In the night sky's theater, there's always much more.
The laughter of planets rings loud and so clear,
In the twilight's embrace, bring the funny and cheer!

## The Language of Distant Skies

In the distance, the stars hold a meeting,
Their twinkling whispers become something fleeting.
A comet comes crashing, a real show-off blend,
With jokes and puns, it just can't see an end.

Galaxies giggle with a flicker and swirl,
While space dust dances, a sparkly twirl.
Each nebula boasts of a joke or a pun,
While black holes grin, saying, "Don't let us run!"

The moons form a choir with Saturn's round rings,
Chorusing laughter while each planet sings.
With echoes of mirth bouncing back from afar,
The universe beams like a giant blue star.

So let's all converse in this stellar ballet,
With the laughter of asteroids lighting the way.
In the cold of the cosmos, a warmth we can find,
With jokes from the heavens to lighten the mind!

## **Starborn Melodies**

In a spaceship of dreams, the crew starts to hum,
With melodies crafted from laughter and fun.
A supernova jives and a quasar swings low,
As galaxies chuckle in light years of glow.

Shooting stars scatter like jokes on the breeze,
While aliens write with a flair that can tease.
They pop cosmic balloons, and the laughter erupts,
As the universe giggles and never interrupts.

The Milky Way winks, sharing secrets at night,
With whimsical wonders that tickle delight.
Each star sings a verse, with a wink and a spin,
Creating a concert, let the laughter begin!

So let's raise a glass of stardust and cheer,
To the whimsical music that we all hold dear.
In the vastness of space, let joy be our guide,
For the dance of the stars is the laughter inside!

## Whims of the Solar System

On the fourth rock from the sun, what a sight,
The planets throw parties every day and night.
Mercury speed-tweets while Venus does spin,
Taking selfies with Earth, all the laughs never thin.

Mars tells a tale of a galactic cheer,
With robots that juggle and comets that leer.
Jupiter laughs with its stormy old grin,
While Saturn's rings play a tune from within.

Uranus is next, with a color parade,
Its dances eccentric, none ever dismayed.
Neptune hums softly, a lullaby tune,
Sharing dreams with the stars under a whimsical moon.

So come join the laughter, don't mind the space,
In the solar system, it's a comical place.
With bytes of pure joy, each orbit a blast,
In the whims of the cosmos, let's party at last!

## A Celestial Gathering of Words

In the cosmos, laughter flies,
Stars wink with playful sighs.
Planets dance in quirky styles,
Jupiter jests, oh how it smiles!

Galaxies spin in merry glee,
Mars teases with its red decree.
Saturn's rings are tossed like confetti,
While comets scribble jokes so petty.

Neptune joins with a giggling sound,
Uranus spins, whirling around.
In this space of jolly spree,
Words tumble like light debris.

Shooting stars are punchlines bright,
Twinkling laughter fills the night.
A cosmic bash for all to share,
Where words are spun into the air!

# **Eclipsed in Verse**

Under the shadow, words collide,
Playful phrases, hats we bide.
With a wink, the sun goes shy,
While moons giggle and roll on by.

Eclipsed in laughter's sweet embrace,
Words leap forth, a frisky chase.
Comets race with jokes to tell,
In a cosmic carnival, all is well.

Puns and rhymes float in the void,
Where every star feels overjoyed.
Tickling tongues, a merry tease,
In this eclipse, we laugh with ease.

With cosmic flair and style galore,
Words dance beneath the astral floor.
Hiding, seeking, in a jest,
In this eclipse, we are truly blessed!

## The Frosty Muse Awakens

In icy realms where snowflakes play,
The muse awakens in a funny way.
With frosty breath, it warms the skies,
Crafting verses that go awry.

Chilling giggles fill the air,
While icy spirits pull your hair.
A snowball poem bounces about,
In frosty fun, we twist and shout.

Icicles drip with whispered cheer,
As frozen jokes draw laughter near.
Creating frost, a quirky rhyme,
Where winter's chill turns into lime.

With every flurry, whimsy glows,
A shivery muse that simply knows.
In a world where fun is bold,
Frosty laughter, a joy to behold.

## Ode to the Unseen Voyager

Through the cosmic sea, it drifts in jest,
An unseen voyager on a funny quest.
With a mischievous wink and a silent cheer,
It whispers tales we long to hear.

With every star, it makes a friend,
Crafting quirks that never end.
A galactic guide in a silly attire,
Sailing through time with giggles to inspire.

Behind the rings, it plays hide and seek,
Sending playful pings, unique and sleek.
A wanderer in comic space,
Where laughter echoes, we embrace.

So here's to the traveler, lost in flight,
Spreading joy in the endless night.
In the cosmos, with humor's tune,
We celebrate this whimsical boon!

## Ballads of Dusk and Discovery

A gathering of oddballs, what a sight!
The stars compete for laughter, so bright.
Moonbeams giggle, comets play tag,
As shadows dance and wiggle, they brag.

Mice in tuxedos, hopping with grace,
Jokes on their tails, a whimsical race.
The sun takes a nap, the night is quite zany,
Laughter echoes, filled with joy so brainy.

Each planet spins tales of silly mishaps,
While asteroids tumble in cushy soft naps.
Eclipses throw parties, craters bring snacks,
And those starlit ballads dance on their tracks.

With stardust confetti floating all around,
The cosmos holds secrets, just waiting to be found.
A toast to the night with giggles galore,
Join the fun, oh friend, there's always more!

## Stanzas Amidst the Stars

In the realm of the twinklers, funny and bright,
Galaxies whisper jokes in the night.
Moony jesters juggling, oh what a feat,
Each word a comet, surprising and sweet.

Starry-eyed poets sip on space tea,
While meteors crack jokes, urging glee.
A supernova's punchline, bursting with flair,
Leaves everyone chuckling, floating in air.

Black holes are shy, but their punchlines are bold,
As planets spin tales that never grow old.
Whirling and twirling, the sun plays a tune,
With laughter galore from the craters of June.

The orbits collide, like confetti they scatter,
In cosmic connection, nothing else matters.
Join in the laughter, let the stardust align,
In the stanzas of space, where giggles entwine.

## The Cosmic Dancer's Lament

In twinkling shoes, the comets do glide,
With starry companions, they swirl and slide.
Bumping their heads on meteor showers,
Each twirl and leap unfolds cosmic power.

Aliens breakdance, their moves quite bizarre,
Flashing their colors, neons from afar.
The sun drags its feet, but shimmies in place,
While planets all chuckle, in laughter they race.

A hiccup of moonlight, a stumble on dust,
Every step sends ripples, oh what a bust!
The asteroid band plays a jingly beat,
And even the craters scamper on feet.

But worry not, friends, for glimmers remain,
As giggles and wobbles flow through the brain.
With cosmic delight, dancing don't wane,
In the vastness, the fun's never plain!

## Frozen Rhymes and Distant Chimes

Out in the cosmos, where cold winds do blow,
Frosty imaginations begin to grow.
Snowflakes are giggling, with icy delight,
As stars tickle tails in the blanket of night.

A chilly old planet, so quiet and shy,
Whispers of humor run deep through the sky.
The comets parade in their frosty attire,
Making snowmen who dance and never tire.

The rings of the giants start clinking with cheer,
Juggling their ice cubes, spread joy far and near.
Frozen rhymes twist in a whimsical flight,
As laughter erupts from the depths of the night.

Distant chimes echo, a symphony's play,
Turning frosty frowns into smiles every day.
In the fun of creation, the universe spins,
With musical wonders where laughter begins.

# A Journey through the Cold Expanse

In a realm where ice is king,
Snowflakes dance, and comets sing,
Traveling through the chilly air,
Who knew space could be such a fair?

A penguin struts with cosmic flair,
His top hat tipped, he doesn't care,
Asteroids laugh as they roll by,
Rehearsing verses in the sky.

Galactic jesters throw their pies,
Saturn's rings echo happy cries,
While Neptune spins a playful tale,
A slippery slope, but never frail.

So raise a glass of Martian fizz,
To frosty fun and cosmic whiz,
Through the cold, we find our cheer,
In the vast expanse, we draw near.

## Musing Among the Planets

Bouncing thoughts from star to star,
Jupiter giggles, oh, what a czar!
Mars throws shade with a wink and grin,
While Mercury scribbles, ready to spin.

Venus winks from a silken cloud,
Gathering laughter from the crowd,
In this cosmic coffee shop affair,
We sip on dreams, with style and flair.

Uranus pipes in with a silly joke,
Even the asteroids gasp and poke,
While the sun cracks up over the brew,
Can laughter really warm up the blue?

So join the fun, the space-age glee,
Each orb spins tales of jubilee,
In a universe where humor reigns,
Musing among the planets, no chains.

**The Faraway Muse**

Faraway worlds call our name,
With a whimsical spark of cosmic flame,
A muse in orbit, spinning round,
In stellar fantasies, joy is found.

Galaxy giggles drift like balloons,
Tickled by interstellar tunes,
A comet's tail twirls like a skirt,
As laughter echoes through the dirt.

With aliens dancing in a line,
Chasing echoes of the divine,
They shuffle past with quirky grace,
Throwing confetti in this odd place.

So when you gaze at the night so clear,
Let the cosmic laughter draw you near,
For in the distance, joy holds sway,
The faraway muse knows how to play.

## **Lyrical Dreams of the Icy Frontier**

Upon the ice, where shadows play,
Lyrical dreams chase blues away,
Frosty verses glide and swirl,
In this chill, creativity unfurls.

With snowmen poets stacking high,
Crafting rhymes to fill the sky,
Each stanza pops like icy fizz,
Who knew cold could be such a whiz?

Riding meteors, sliding through,
The icy frontier's a wondrous view,
While cosmic critters hum and sway,
To melodies of a frozen ballet.

So gather 'round this frosty ball,
As laughter echoes past the sprawl,
In lyrical dreams, we take flight,
Through the ice, we'll dance all night.

## Cosmic Ballad of the Frozen Heart

In the dark where comets zoom,
A snowman danced in shadowed gloom.
He lost his hat, it flew away,
Now he can't find it, what a day!

The stars above just laugh and shine,
As he stumbles on the icy line.
His carrot nose begins to freeze,
What a sight to bring you to your knees!

A rocket ship whirls past a star,
Chasing dreams, oh, how bizarre!
The snowman waved, he felt so bold,
But his icy limbs were turning cold.

With frozen feet, he starts to glide,
Through cosmic snow, he takes a ride.
Amidst the ice, he sings with cheer,
In this grand void, he has no fear.

## Shadows in the Kuiper Belt

In the shadows, munching ice cream,
Small planets plot their cosmic scheme.
One whispers low, 'Let's play a game!'
The others giggle without shame.

They race on rings made of old dust,
With tiny rockets, they zoom, they gust.
But oops! One tripped, and down he flew,
His ice cream flew and splattered too!

A lonely comet watched with glee,
As friends transformed to jubilee.
They laughed and danced, their joy so bright,
In the chilly dark, what a delight!

The Kuiper Belt, a playground vast,
With silly antics, they'll have a blast.
As they twirl under starlit sights,
They find pure joy in frosty nights.

## A Dance with Icy Realms

In the realm of frost and cheer,
The planets gather, drawing near.
With ice skates made from moonbeams bright,
They glide and laugh through starry night.

A giant's foot slips on the ice,
He lands with a thud, quite precise!
The little ones all stop and stare,
Then burst with giggles everywhere.

One spins round, a cosmic whirl,
With twinkling lights, they give a twirl.
They trade their hats, they trade some fun,
Under the gaze of the glowing sun.

With icy breath, they shout with glee,
Come join the dance; we're wild and free!
In realms of chill, they'll dance till dawn,
Across the void, their joys live on.

## The Secrets of the Dwarf Planet

Deep within, a secret lies,
Of laughter shared beneath the skies.
A hidden jest, a cosmic feast,\nWhere planets party, to say the least!

They coalesce in joyful glee,
Telling tales of stardust spree.
One whispers soft, "I found a joke,"
With every line, more laughter woke.

The frozen moons join in the fun,
With playful tricks, they dash and run.
They swap their rings for silly hats,
In this great void, where laughs are at!

As laughter echoes, comets crash,
And party hats begin to flash.
In every wink, a secret shared,
In icy realms, they've all prepared.

## The Poet's Voyage through the Dark

In a ship made of words, I sailed so bright,
Finding rhymes in the shadows, oh what a sight!
With metaphors twinkling like stars in the night,
I bumped into commas, they gave me a fright!

I chatted with nouns that danced on the breeze,
While verbs were all giggling, aiming to tease.
I tripped over adverbs, they fell to their knees,
And laughed till I cried, searching for keys.

The moon offered stanzas, all shiny and new,
A chorus of cosmos, with verses to chew.
Seductive sonnets in silvery hues,
Gave birth to ballads that humorously woo.

As I paddled through puns in the chocolatey dark,
I scribbled some lines, each one a wild spark.
In laughter we erupted, oh what a lark,
With cosmic giggles illuminating the stark!

## Poetry in the Deep Blue

In an ocean of lines, I dived with delight,
Where the fishes recited their rhymes every night.
Octopuses scribbled, their ink flowing bright,
While clams clapped in rhythm, oh what a sight!

Coral reefs chuckled with colors so bold,
Their tales of adventure were waiting to be told.
I penned down the laughter, a treasure to hold,
As seahorses pranced, their stories unrolled.

With tides of octaves, I surfed on a wave,
Finding humor in kelp, it was all I could save.
The dolphins narrated in tones both brave,
And each splash was a stanza, my spirits they gave!

As I floated on laughter, from gullible lines,
The depths of the ocean were bursting with signs.
I danced with the currents, their rhythms divine,
In the blue of the sea, where fun always shines!

**Frigid Fancies of the Far Universe**

In the cold of the cosmos, where giggles ignite,
I spun around planets, a dazzling sight.
With snowflakes of syllables swirling in flight,
I ushered in laughter to banish the night.

With a comet for a quill, I scribbled with flair,
Where frostbitten stanzas floated in air.
The icebergs were critiquing, a frosty affair,
While penguins applauded with flair beyond compare.

The stars winked and chuckled, the moons spun their lies,

I gathered the humor from the milky white skies.
With a giggle explosion, my spirit did rise,
In the chill of the universe, creativity flies!

As I skated on rhymes, in a cosmic ballet,
The universe chuckled, it joined in the play.
With laughter and whimsy lighting the way,
In the farthest of realms, I found joy every day!

## Whirlwind of Cosmic Wonder

In a whirlwind of words, I twirled with delight,
Chasing comets and rhymes, a fanciful flight.
Through black holes of humor, I danced with the night,
Making friends with the stardust, all merry and bright.

Planets popped popcorn, their rings spun so sweet,
While galaxies giggled with each little beat.
I caught cosmic jokes like candy to eat,
In the swirling expanse, fun tasted like heat.

With a bounce on my toes, I juggled with stars,
While asteroids winked, sharing tales from afar.
Their humor was witty, it shone like guitars,
In this silly ballet on cosmic memoirs.

So I laughed with the nebulae, curving my grin,
As I soared through the tales, the wonders within.
With a twist in the fabric, where giggles begin,
I spun through the universe, joy buried in sin!

## Radiant Whispers from the Twilight Zone

In the dark, where shadows play,
A squirrel with shades takes the stage.
He juggles acorns with great flair,
While moonbeams giggle in midair.

The stars are clapping, what a sight!
As comets join in, feeling bright.
Alien cats dance on their tails,
In this cosmic circus, fun prevails!

Laughter echoes through the night,
With every burst, the world feels light.
A quasar sings of silly dreams,
In very earnest, bright moonbeams.

So grab a seat, and join the cheer,
For space has humor, never fear.
In this zone where whispers roam,
You'll find the joy that feels like home.

## Harmonies from the Cosmic Abyss

Down in the depths where stars collide,
An octopus plays, full of pride.
With eight-armed flair, he plucks the strings,
And sultry melodies he brings.

The black holes spin with a funky beat,
While dancing planets shuffle their feet.
A unicorn trots, not a care at all,
In this abyss, we have a ball!

Rhythm floats on hydrogen waves,
As space-time twists with cosmic raves.
Neutron stars tap their little toes,
In a place where laughter flows.

So come right down to the groove, my friend,
Where silly songs will never end.
In the abyss, the joy won't cease,
Here in the groove, we find our peace.

## Tales of the Dwarfed and Distant

Once upon a time, in a tiny sphere,
Dwarfs told tales that drew us near.
They spun the yarns of cosmic quests,
In slippers soft, they made their nests.

A gnome who danced atop a star,
Claimed to know the world's bizarre.
With marshmallow rockets, they'd zoom and sway,
In a sparkly caper, they'd save the day!

From distant moons, the laughter rang,
As each little story took to slang.
With feathered quills they wrote with glee,
In their world of wonders, bright and free.

So let us cheer for tales well told,
From tiny folk, both brave and bold.
In the vast universe, a truth outshines,
In every heartbeat, humor entwines.

## **Rhymes Beneath the Outer Rim**

Underneath the starry dome,
The aliens craft a cheeky poem.
With words that tickle and make you grin,
They rhyme of mischief where fun begins.

With cosmic dust, they write in haste,
About a planet shaped like a face.
A silly giant with feet too big,
Who takes a tumble doing a jig!

Comets race, trying to rhyme,
With every twist, they slip through time.
A kangaroo hops in on the beat,
In this wacky world, they can't be beat!

So join the fun as we rhyme and cheer,
With silly whispers that all can hear.
Beneath the rim where laughter grows,
In this delightful space, anything goes!

## **Starry Eyed Soliloquy**

I danced with a comet, oh what a sight,
It twirled and it whirled in the velvety night.
My jokes were tremendous, I spat them with glee,
Even the asteroids chuckled, 'A star's jubilee!'

The moons were all laughing, their eyes full of shine,
While meteors joked, 'Hey, that punchline's divine!'
I offered a star a joke, fresh out of the box,
He winked and he grinned, 'You sure crack some rocks!'

Octopus nebulae rolled in the light,
Telling tall tales of their travels in flight.
I gathered my verses, my rhymes in a hat,
Shared laughs with my friends, 'How about that!'

So raise up your glasses, a toast to the fun,
Dancing with stardust till the night is done.
With laughter and verses, we'll travel afar,
In the midst of the cosmos, we're the shining stars!

## Verses from a Distant Shore

On a moon made of cheese, what a curious thing,
I found a small turtle who served me a drink.
He talked of the galaxies, wild and so free,
And shared his best puns, oh, they tickled me!

I launched into poetry, breezy and bright,
Words floated around like balloons in the night.
My verses flew off like they had wings to soar,
While the starfish yelled, 'Encore! More! More!'

There's laughter in space where the comets all play,
With friends from the stars, we'll dance night and day.
With each rhyme I spun, the nebulae swayed,
At this party of stardust, I'm happily swayed.

A starfish in shades caught a wave of my words,
While crabs in tuxedos tapped beats like the birds.
On this jovial shore, we're all poets at heart,
Crafting cosmic verses, let the fun never part!

## The Heartbeat of a Lonely Planet

In the depths of the void, where the silence is loud,
A planet sat sulking, alone in a cloud.
I whispered some secrets to give it some cheer,
And soon it was giggling, 'I like it out here!'

With quarks and with quirks, I shared silly tales,
As it spun and it twirled on its imaginary rails.
Quasars chimed in, with a laugh and a wink,
'You're not so alone, come on, let's all drink!'

The universe whispered, 'There's fun to be found,
In the quirks of your heart, let your laughter abound!'
So I danced with the shadows that fluttered like bees,
While the lonely old planet spun happy with ease.

Now the beat of the cosmos is vibrant and bright,
Forging friendships in darkness with shimmering light.
With every soft giggle, it's clear to perceive,
That joy can be found, if you dare to believe!

## Chasing Shadows in the Dark

With starlight as my lantern, I wandered the night,
Chasing shadows of dreams, oh what a delight!
They giggled and dashed, slipping under my feet,
'Catch us if you can, it's a lingering feat!'

I tripped on a bright meteor, fell in a laugh,
The echoes of giggles were nearly a gaffe.
But comets had joined in, with raucous uproar,
As the darkness erupted with fun evermore!

A black hole said softly, 'Don't take life too stark,
Let's paint the universe with your finest remark!'
So I filled up my balloons with verses and quips,
Then watched all the shadows take fabulous trips.

As the night turned to day with a wink and a spin,
I waved goodbye to the giggles, my heart full of gin.
For in chasing the shadows, we learn, it's a lark,
That laughter and joy can ignite any dark!

## The Enchanted Silence of the Cosmos

In the dark where shadows play,
Comets dance, then zoom away.
Planets giggle, stars in tow,
Whispers float where nebulae glow.

Asteroids bounce like clumsy fools,
Orbiting in cosmic schools.
A black hole hiccups, quite a sight,
As stardust chuckles through the night.

Aliens pick up cosmic chats,
Trading tales like silly bats.
They rhyme with moons in frosty beams,
Creating laughter from their dreams.

Galaxies swirl in joyous spins,
In this space, the giggle begins.
Each twinkle is a wink from fate,
In the silence, stars can't wait.

## Legendary Echoes from the Dark Side

On the dark side, jokes abound,
Where the weird and funny are found.
Rockets toast with fizzy drinks,
As satellites share their quirky winks.

Martians play pranks, hide and seek,
Tickling moons with laughter so chic.
Orbiting stars make quite a scene,
Chasing dreams through the cosmic green.

Astro-snails play hopscotch slow,
While cosmic bunnies steal the show.
Each echo bounces like a tune,
Underneath the watchful moon.

Supernovae burst like laughter's might,
Painting the canvas of the night.
When darkness chuckles, you must cheer,
For space is fun, nowhere near fear.

## Whispers of the Distant World

Far away in a twinkling zone,
Little stars laugh on their throne.
They chat in colors, red and blue,
Whispering tales of things they do.

They gossip about comets' flights,
And tease about the meteors' bites.
With giggles echoing through the vast,
Space laughs hard, it's quite a blast!

Nebulas send out puffy sighs,
While planets wink with glowing eyes.
"Did you see that?" they all shout,
As satellites tumble about.

With each chuckle, stardust thrives,
Creating magic in funny lives.
In the night, joy takes its form,
As the universe spins and warms.

## Celestial Verses Beneath the Stars

Beneath the stars, a party's bright,
Where planets quirk and laugh outright.
Comets strut with tails of flair,
All the cosmos joins to share.

In this fest of twinkling sights,
Asteroids skate, oh what delights!
Galaxies giggle, bursting wide,
In this joyful galactic ride.

Voices echo through the spheres,
Trading laughs and cosmic cheers.
Each star shines with a joyful glow,
In this celestial cabaret show.

With each tick of time, they sing,
A humorous tune on cosmic string.
In the vastness, love and jest,
The universe feels at its best.

## Ode to the Twilight Horizon

In the twilight where shadows dance,
Little comets twirl in a cosmic chance.
Aliens chuckle as they munch on stars,
Sipping moonlight from their candy jars.

The sun winks while planets play tag,
Eclipsing each other, they bravely brag.
A cosmic game on a galactic stage,
Where laughter ripples like an endless wave.

Rings of Saturn, a circus of rings,
Jupiter sings as the melody swings.
Neptune giggles, wearing a crown of mist,
Saying, "Join us, you simply can't resist!"

So dance with the asteroids, jive with the dust,
In this twilight realm, oh, we must!
With humor and joy as our guiding light,
Let's celebrate this galactic night!

## Galactic Rhapsody of the Edge

At the edge of the cosmos, oh what a sight,
Shooting stars play hopscotch under the night.
Galactic giggles echo far and wide,
As aliens prance, their joy cannot hide.

In zero gravity, they float and they spin,
Tripping on stardust, they're bound to win.
Every twinkle's a laugh, each flash a joke,
While comets conspire to tickle and poke.

Meteor showers rain down with flair,
Dancing meteors, do they even care?
They splash cosmic paint on the velvet sky,
Creating a canvas where laughter can fly.

So gather around, for the show is grand,
With giggles and grins from this cosmic band.
In this rhapsody, joy becomes our song,
At the edge of the night, where we all belong.

## Echoes from the Outer Rim

In the outer rim, where echoes bounce,
Whispers of laughter make the starlight prounce.
Galaxies giggle with a twinkle of grace,
As comets all gather for a silly race.

Beyond the rocks, where adventures unfold,
Gravity's tricks are pure cosmic gold.
Asteroids chuckle as they whirl around,
Every spin makes a jest, profound.

Uranus spins with a quirky grin,
Pretending to lose while actually in.
Mercury zips with a giggle so bold,
Each movement a story waiting to be told.

So let the stars sing of joy and cheer,
With echoes of fun that we hold dear.
In this outer realm, where dreams take flight,
We dance with laughter, shining bright.

## **Stardust Serenade**

In a cosmic café where the stardust flows,
Planets sip merrily from galactic prose.
A space-time serenade, oh what a delight,
As meteors croon under the soft moonlight.

Asteroids jive with a swing and a twist,
Creating a rhythm, you can't resist.
Neon nebulae sparkle, a colorful spree,
Inviting us in for a cosmic cup of tea.

Galaxies twirl in their swirling delight,
While Saturn's rings gleam with joy, so bright.
Singing the songs of the wide-open void,
In this stardust realm, we can't help but be excited.

So raise your glasses to the stars above,
In this serenade, we find our love.
Where laughter echoes through the cosmic sea,
Let's dance through the night, just you and me!

## An Invitation to Cosmic Stillness

Join us where the stars align,
In slippers made of space and time.
We'll sip on comets, dance with glee,
Under a sky that's wide and free.

Bring your quirkiest thoughts to share,
We'll float like balloons, light as air.
With giggles bouncing from Mars to Venus,
Let's create a cosmos that's truly keenest.

Asteroids might join in the groove,
While cosmic dust begins to move.
Strange snacks from the Moon will appear,
Lunar cheese wheels, grab a sphere!

So polish your space boots, it's a blast,
We'll laugh 'til the stars seem unsurpassed.
With tales of black holes and alien jokes,
Don't miss out on the fun, dear folks!

## Frosty Whispers in the Galactic Dawn

Morning comes with frosty breath,
Chilly giggles that dance with depth.
Snowflakes shaped like tiny stars,
Winking down from Jupiter's bars.

We'll skate on rings made of icy bliss,
Each twirl a twist, we can't resist.
In the glow of a stellar light,
We'll tickle the comets, oh what a sight!

Giggling meteors zoom on by,
In their wake, we'll reach for the sky.
A snowman built from cosmic fluff,
With a carrot nose and laughter enough.

So don your mittens, let's collide,
With frosty whispers that will abide.
This party's not just 'out of this world',
It's where the snowflakes unfurl!

## **The Uncharted Meander of Space**


Wandering through the starry maze,
Where gravity loses all its ways.
Planets tumble in a playful race,
In the grand game of cosmic chase.

Each comet's tail is a silly joke,
Sending giggles as they poke and stroke.
Galactic giggles, bright and vast,
In this uncharted realm, let's have a blast!

Join a nebula for a cheeky chat,
With a twinkly wink and a feathered hat.
We'll hop on asteroids, bounce and spin,
Laughing loud as we take it all in.

With every turn, a surprise awaits,
In the cosmic dance of the celestial states.
So grab your friends, don't be late,
To meander in the fun, it's first-rate!

## **Verses on the Edge of Existence**

On the edge where laughter blooms,
Beyond the shadows and cosmic glooms.
We'll spin our stories with endless cheer,
In unity, we'll conquer the fear.

Galactic giggles echo through time,
As we explore the universe's rhyme.
Each verse an adventure, wild and bright,
On the edge of existence, we shine our light.

With every quasar, a new punchline,
Connecting stars, their shimmer divine.
Let's write our poems in stellar dust,
In this vast expanse, we find our trust.

So bring your humor, your whims, your fun,
Together we'll blaze like a neutron sun.
In rhymes of existence, together we'll sing,
As the universe dances, we spread our wings!

## Distant Echoes of Celestial Chords

In the darkness, where spacecats play,
A comet sneezes, sending stars astray.
Galactic giggles ring through the void,
As planets dance, all drama destroyed.

Moons move in rhythm, a cosmic parade,
With meteor showers, the grand charade.
Asteroids juggling, how silly it seems,
While aliens sip on their stardust dreams.

Wormholes whisper, secrets they tell,
One says, 'Earth's just a lousy hotel!'
While quasars chuckle, lighting the gloom,
In this starry circus, there's always room.

So join in the laughter, let starlight ignite,
In the cosmic jokes, the universe bright.
For in every echo, a chorus we find,
Distant and funny, to lighten the mind.

## **Wandering through Starlit Truths**

Lost in the cosmos, where time drips slow,
A neutron star wrestles a black hole's glow.
Galaxies spin in their silly ballet,
Chasing their tails like it's fun to play.

Gravity giggles as comets race by,
While moons tell tales to the twinkling sky.
With each little hiccup, a supernova roars,
As stars swap stories of cosmic pursuits.

Light-years of laughter echo through space,
In the heart of the void, there's always a place.
For whimsical wonders from around the bend,
In this universe wild, the fun never ends.

So twirl with the planets, and spin with the stars,
In the fabric of space, let's sing with guitars.
With each strum we travel, through truths freshly brewed,

In the laughter of galaxies, our spirits renewed.

## **A Tapestry of Celestial Dreams**

Weaving stardust into threads so bright,
Sewing wishes under the moon's soft light.
With cosmic yarn, we craft and we spin,
Holding tight to the laughter, the joy within.

Planets jostle for the best view near,
While shooting stars race, fueled by their cheer.
A tapestry glimmers with colors galore,
In this wacky universe, who could ask for more?

Nebulae puff like cotton candy skies,
While moons make faces that elicit sighs.
The sun cracks jokes, warming up the scene,
In this vibrant quilt, absurd and serene.

So come join this dance on a comet's tail,
With giggles and grins, we'll set off to sail.
In the weave of the cosmos, let laughter take flight,
For dreams spun in starlight are truly a sight.

## **Voices in the Solar Wind**

In the whispers of solar breezes we hear,
Jokes told by light, both silly and clear.
The planets respond with a comical shout,
While asteroids nod, their laughter devout.

A sunbeam winks as it skips through the night,
Making drapes of laughter with beams of delight.
As rockets zoom past, they wave with a grin,
In the playful embrace of the universe's spin.

The stars are the audience, twinkling mirth,
Each nova a punchline, each quasar's birth.
Oh, how the cosmos dances in glee,
In this infinite jest, we are wild and free.

So listen closely, let the echoes unwind,
For in this vast theater, joy's easy to find.
With voices that travel through space and through time,
The laughter of starlight, eternally chimes.

## The Unseen Poet of the Solar Wind

In the shadows of the cosmos, he scribbles with glee,
A cosmic quill spinning tales, floating free.
Stars giggle and twinkle, they giggle aloud,
As he rhymes with the planets, he's cheeky and proud.

His parchment's made of comets, dust, and bright flair,
He jots down his verses while dancing in air.
With a wink and a twist, he sends words afar,
Like a leaf in the breeze, or a bright shooting star.

With each swirl of stardust, a joke comes to light,
Galaxies chuckle, what a whimsical sight!
He honors the silence, yet teases the void,
This poet unseen, is playful and coy.

So raise up your glasses to things that you can't see,
To the whimsy of orbits and cosmic debris!
For laughter's the language of all that we know,
And the unseen poet won't steal the show!

## Rhymes from the Ninth Orbit

From the edge of the solar system, they twirl and they spin,
Where the light starts to dim, but the fun's still within.
Planets all gather, dressed up for the scene,
Tasked with creating a rhyming cuisine.

With a whirl and a pop, the gas giants laugh,
They bounce to the rhythm, split joy in half.
Asteroids chuckle, with a clink and a clank,
As meteors pass by, like a prank on the plank.

Neptune's caught rhyming, while Saturn sings low,
Their verses spin forward, and then to and fro.
Orbits are huddled in giggles and blooms,
As galaxies echo with poetic costumes.

Each word floats like bubbles, bursting with fun,
From the ninth orbit's party, never to shun.
So join in the laughter, let the cosmos decide,
That rhymes from the ninth orbit are something we bide!

## **Frosted Dreams of the Dark Side**

Under blankets of ice, where the shadows reside,
The party erupts, a wild cosmic ride.
Frosted dreams twinkle, in a chilly embrace,
As laughter erupts in this far-off place.

Sneaky moons giggle as they twirl in the frost,
Sharing glimmers of humor, no joy is lost.
With icy zingers, like snowflakes they land,
A tickle of frosty, a whimsical hand.

Through the darkness they twinkle, the stars play along,
With echoes of laughter, they mimic the song.
Dreams of the frost give a soft little shove,
To warm up the hearts, and remind us of love.

So dance in the chill, let the laughter ring out,
On the dark side of dreams, there's no room for doubt.
With frosted delights and an icy good cheer,
Let's revel in poetry, warmth cuddles near!

## Celestial Reflections in the Void

In the vast empty spaces, where silence does dwell,
Reflective whispers spin, weaving a spell.
Stars converse softly, exchanging a wink,
While galaxies chuckle, more than you think.

Through voids they wander, their jokes on repeat,
With a cosmic twist that's utterly sweet.
Light years away, they still share a grin,
Galactic reflections, let the fun begin!

Echoes of laughter break barriers wide,
In the whimsical depths where the secrets abide.
As planets take jabs at the comets that pass,
Their humor cascades in a cosmic morass.

So join in the giggles, let your spirit fly,
In the celestial realm where we reach for the sky.
For reflections in voids are so grand and so bright,
With laughter as stardust, they light up the night!

## Transcendent Tales of the Night

In the dark of space, we toss and we twirl,
Stars wear their hats, and galaxies swirl.
A comet slides by, just a wink and a grin,
Who knew cosmic events could start with a spin?

Aliens dance with a wiggly groove,
They boogie in stardust, that's how they move.
With donuts and coffee served on a moon,
They're jiving beneath a most humorous tune.

Black holes are friendly, they giggle and play,
Spinning out laughter at the end of the day.
A wormhole hiccup sends time on a run,
Back to the start, oh what funny fun!

So gather your friends 'round the cosmic release,
For tales of the night bring a chuckle and peace.
With jokes like asteroids tumbling down,
We'll laugh through the cosmos without a frown.

## Spheres of Silence and Song

In the vacuum of space, whispers float by,
Where planets debate if they're shy or they try.
A moon with a sax, plays solo and smooth,
While Mars cracks a joke, hoping to groove.

Neptune's a comedian telling some tales,
While Saturn just spins with his glittery veils.
Venus rolls on, she's a fun-loving gal,
With laughter that echoes like a bright cosmic ball.

Stars shoot across skies, with wishes and dreams,
While galaxies giggle in soft, swirling beams.
A one-eyed creature from a distant old scrap,
Jumps in for a laugh, with a giddy old clap.

So join in the harmony, the laughter and light,
In these spheres of silence, let's share our delight.
With melodies spinning, and joy floating high,
We'll dance through the cosmos, just you and I.

## Intergalactic Harmonies

Whirling in space where the silence is gold,
Together we spin tales, both funny and bold.
A starry-eyed puppet pulls strings of delight,
As comets join in on this whimsical night.

Asteroids clatter, like marbles on floors,
They giggle around when they bump into doors.
A singing space whale belts out a sweet tune,
As meteors whisper secrets of the moon.

While quasars twinkle with a mischievous spark,
A cosmic joke echoes, hitting the mark.
Lunar llamas prance, with fireworks in tow,
Hosting a bash in the shades of a glow.

So join this vast gathering of laughter and cheer,
A festival of humor, no worries, no fear.
With intergalactic harmonies booming in flight,
Let's celebrate the cosmos, in joyous delight!

## A Symphony of the Unseen


The universe hums an enchanting bass line,
Though most can't hear it, it's simply divine.
Stars pull their strings while black holes swoon,
Creating a rhythm upon the night's tune.

With vibes from the void, they dance and collide,
Each planet seasoned with laughter and pride.
A jester named Mercury spins on a dime,
While bringing the chuckles, he's quite the sublime.

Jupiter laughs, with his stormy embrace,
As Saturn's rings twinkle, he shows off his grace.
The milky waves ripple, a dance on the floor,
Where stardust meets laughter, asking for more.

In this hidden concert, we twirl and we sway,
To a symphony unseen, that brightens the fray.
So tune in your heart to the humor and cheer,
The universe is laughing, so let's all draw near!

www.ingramcontent.com/pod-product-compliance
Lightning Source LLC
Chambersburg PA
CBHW071850160426
43209CB00003B/491